10 Simple Habits

for a

Happier Life

Lynda K. Giddens

HUMMINGBIRD NORTHWEST

SEATTLE

Copyright © 2014 by Lynda K. Giddens

All rights reserved.

No part of this publication may be reproduced, distributed, or transmitted in any form or by any means, including photocopying, recording, or other electronic or mechanical methods, without the prior written permission of the publisher, except in the case of brief quotations embodied in critical reviews and certain other noncommercial uses permitted by copyright law.

ISBN 978-0-9905727-1-8

Publisher: Hummingbird Northwest

Illustrated by Cassie Peng

For my nephew, Ben.

May you live happily ever after.

Introduction

There are lots of things that might seem to determine whether or not you are happy: How much money you have, how hard you have to work, how healthy you are, what family support and/or issues you have, etc. While all of those things can have an effect on your happiness, they don't have to determine how happy you are.

You determine how happy you are—in any situation.

The good news is that it isn't very hard to do, and I can teach you how.

The ten habits covered in this book are the fundamentals for creating a happier life for yourself. There are more things you can do that will be covered in future books, but these are the basics. This is where you need to start.

I call them "simple" because no preparation is required, and they don't take much time to do. You can easily fit them into your daily routine.

I call them habits because they are much more a way of life rather than a series of steps you take or projects you complete. Like all habits, they need to be developed through repetition.

Practice these habits every day and before you know it, you'll be living a much happier life—and so will everyone around you!

Disclaimer

This book is not designed to be a cure for real depression, diagnosed or not. If you suspect that you might be clinically depressed, or if the idea of attempting any of these habits seems overwhelming, please seek professional help right away.

Habit #1

Celebrate Your Successes

Celebrating your successes helps you to feel good about yourself, which is a key requirement for living a happier life.

Most of us are pretty good at celebrating the big things, but those don't happen very often. That means that we don't get to feel good about ourselves very often. So, I believe it is important to celebrate the small successes, too.

For instance, did you get out of your nice, warm, cozy bed this morning much earlier than you would have liked? If so, that took some initiative on your part and, therefore, counts as an accomplishment. So, congratulate yourself! I do this all the time. Sometimes, especially on a really tough morning, I even raise my arms in triumph and exclaim to myself, "I did it!"

Imagine how much brighter *your* day would be if you started it off feeling like a winner!

Did you get the kids off to school on time today? Applause please!

Did you get to work on time? Take a bow!

Did you remember to stop at the store on the way home? Good job!

When you think about it, life is made up of hundreds of little accomplishments like those. Taking them for granted is like saying they don't matter. They *do* matter. These are the things that make you who you are. Stand up and take credit. You deserve it!

You probably experience many other, more significant, successes every day that you don't even recognize because they are disguised as failures. Here is a common example of that:

You start the day with ten items on your to-do list but only get through five of them. Instead of focusing on the five things you didn't do, give yourself credit for the five things you *did* complete. Also, don't forget all of the extra things that came up during the day that interfered with your to-do list. You handled those things just fine. That counts! All of the good stuff counts! Celebrate it!

Why is this celebration stuff important?

At the very least, it can help lighten your mood. (It is very difficult to keep a straight face while congratulating yourself for getting out of bed.)

More importantly, how we view ourselves has a tremendous impact on how we see the world. Simply put, when you feel better about yourself, the world around you seems better, too.

Finally, feeling successful increases your energy level and helps you to feel more confident about your abilities. That inevitably leads to more success—and more happiness!

Habit #2

Look on the Bright Side

You might think that you have to have a happy life before you can look on the bright side of it, but it is actually the other way around. Looking on the bright side of any situation changes your view of that situation. Do it often enough and it changes your view of life.

Here is an example of how that works:

One day last year, I met a guy in the elevator. Both of us had just come in from outside. It was pouring down rain. He was much wetter than I was, so he had obviously been out in the rain much longer. In an attempt to make conversation, I said something like "It's mighty wet outside." He responded, "Yes, it is, but at least it isn't snowing or really cold. I'll take this weather any time over that stuff!" Notice that he didn't complain about the rain or about being wet. He was too busy *looking on the bright side!*

When you do that, the first thing that happens is that you put the current issue in perspective. All of a sudden, being soaking wet doesn't seem so bad. Take that one step further and you're actually feeling lucky that it isn't snowing or cold. That brings us to the real benefit of looking on the bright side. Every time you do that, you are ever so subtly shifting your thinking from feeling unlucky to feeling lucky. Imagine how much happier your life would be if you felt lucky all of the time!

Here are some other situations and possible corresponding bright side responses:

- Hard to get out of bed this morning? *Remind yourself that you get to sleep in on Saturday.*
- Forget your lunch today? *This will give you a chance to try that new sandwich shop!*
- Bus feeling too crowded? *It least you got on...better than having to wait in the cold for the next one!*

See how this works?

I deliberately chose relatively minor issues for my examples because looking on the bright side is a habit that has to be developed. It might be more difficult to apply it to really big things in the beginning. Once you develop the habit, though, you can apply it to more and more situations. Then, before you know it, you are feeling like life is really good *regardless of what happens to you.*

Try it yourself and see how much happier your life can be!

Habit #3

Reframe Your Self-Talk

It is practically impossible to feel good about life when you don't feel good about yourself. And, it is very difficult to feel good about yourself if you've got someone dissing you all the time—especially if that someone is YOU! Yes, it is true; we are often our own worst critic.

Think about it. Most of us have learned (hopefully) the damage that can be done by calling a child "ugly" or "fat" or "stupid." Yet how many of us call ourselves those very same names?

Don't do that to yourself! People, including you, respond much better to positive reinforcement than criticism.

Resolve today to stop calling yourself disparaging names, including the more subtle ones like "lazy," "klutz," "dork," "selfish," etc. If you find yourself about to do that, stop and ask yourself why you deserve this label. Chances are that you just did something that you think fits this description. Take selfish. Were you really being selfish or just doing the best you could at the time? (There is a difference, you know.) Even if you determine that it was selfish, it doesn't mean that *you* are selfish. You've probably done a million unselfish things during the course of your life. Don't allow this one thing—or the others that usually come up when you think about it—to define you. Even if you can't talk yourself out of feeling bad about the action, try rephrasing your self-talk to focus on the action. That is, instead of saying "I am selfish," say "That was a selfish thing to do." That is much less damaging to your self-image.

Along these same lines, don't be so hard on yourself when you make a mistake. I know; you probably think you are supposed to be better than that. The truth is, *everyone* makes mistakes. Whenever you make one, try to correct it if you can, resolve to learn from it, and move on.

Too many of us also discount all of the generous, competent, and kind things we do; as if those things shouldn't matter because they are the norm. They do matter! In fact, they should matter more if they are the norm, since that means that we are normally generous, competent, and kind! Start paying attention to the many things that you do right every day and give yourself credit for them. This positive reinforcement will not only help you to feel better about yourself, it will also make it easier for you to do more good things.

Habit #4

Count Your Blessings

Counting your blessings is not a new concept. Why is it recommended and why does it lead to a happier life? The basic idea is that it forces you to focus on the good things in your life instead of the bad. That will help you to feel more fortunate and give you a brighter perspective about your current situation and the future.

The real key to success with this principle is in the details. Most people think only about the big stuff when they go to count their blessings: health, wealth, family, friends, etc. Those are certainly important, but they are almost too big to have practical application to our daily lives. For one thing, it doesn't take a lot of focus to rattle off the big things. For another, it doesn't help much when you are dealing with concrete issues, such as learning that your car needs a new clutch, for instance.

So, here's what I recommend: Take some time each morning—and more often, if needed—to focus on the *little* blessings of the day before. What do I mean by the little blessings? Here are a few examples of my blessings from the last week:

- Sunny days (We don't take those for granted in Seattle!)
- Finding the perfect skirt at a reasonable price for an upcoming wedding
- An exuberant "I love you!" in an email from a long-time friend
- Checks in the mail (for my business)

This is just a sampling. I can usually come up with at least five things every morning and some of them, like checks in the mail, might occur several times a week. The important thing is to take the time each day to go back through the last 24 hours to look for those blessings and acknowledge them. It will help you to feel better about your daily life and more optimistic about the future.

How do you apply this concept when things aren't going so well? The truth is, we are all "blessed" with good experiences and bad experiences every day. The car repair issue I mentioned above recently happened to me. I could have let it ruin my day, but I decided not to. I focused on the fact that I had a very relaxing and enjoyable day before I learned this news, that I found the perfect skirt, that the sun was shining, and that the deluxe turkey cranberry sandwich I had for lunch was delicious.

How can those seemingly small joys make up for having to schedule a very expensive car repair? It is not about balancing things out. Some days will always be better than others. There isn't anything you can do about that. What you can do, though, is *shift your focus.*

I promise you that if you take the time to look for blessings, you will find them, and if you take the time to acknowledge and savor them, you will feel better about your life. That will make for a happier YOU and make those around you happier, too.

Habit #5

Get Enough Sleep

This may be the hardest habit to keep in our sleep-deprived society, but it is essential to living a happier life.

How much sleep is enough? It varies for each individual, but you need to be rested enough that you can think clearly without so much caffeine that it makes you jittery or anxious. Also, if you start to fall asleep while sitting up after the caffeine wears off, you are probably sleep-deficient.

Why is sleep so important? You have to be able to think clearly to see possibilities and appreciate the humor in life. Also, it takes a fair amount of energy to make good choices and exert the discipline required to follow through on those choices. These things are very difficult to do if you are too tired to focus on anything except putting one foot in front of the other.

If you are having trouble figuring out where to squeeze in that extra sleep time, here are a few suggestions:

- Record your favorite late shows and watch them on the weekend or early the next evening.
- Consider squeezing in naps where possible.
- Start by just going to bed 15 minutes earlier each night. Try that for a week or two and then see if you can add another 15 minutes (and so on, if needed).
- If all else fails, catch up on the weekends.

Getting enough sleep gives you the strength and energy to make good choices and practice good habits. Even better, it helps you feel good, and when you feel good, you are just naturally happier!

Habit #6

Don't Take It Personally

It is very difficult to avoid being affected by the negative emotions, expressions, and actions and inactions of those around us. It is even more difficult when we assume that behavior is either directed at us or is the result of something we've done. The truth is, it is often not about us.

For instance, how often have you felt slighted by people who didn't return phone calls or respond to your texts or emails? Do you worry that this means they don't like you or wish you'd avoid texting or calling? Although that could be the reason, it is much more likely that:

- They didn't know they were expected to respond. (Does "Have a great day" really require a response?)
- They missed the text or message notification because it came in the midst of another communication and maybe didn't get flagged.
- They've been swamped with work or had their phone off and haven't had a chance to respond yet.

None of these reasons have anything to do with you!

Have you ever had someone look at you disapprovingly for seemingly no reason at all? Maybe it was a clerk at the grocery store, a neighbor, or worse yet, your boss. I had been managing people for twenty years before I found out about my *accidental* disapproving look:

> I have a bad habit of scrunching up my forehead when I am evaluating options, and I now know that this appears to be a look of disapproval. I spend a lot of my time at work evaluating options—especially when my employees come to me for advice on a technical issue. Can you imagine how many of my employees went home at night thinking I disapproved of them when all I was doing was thinking!

Do you have people in your life who give you disapproving looks that might not be disapproving, after all?

What if it isn't just a look? What if your partner is grumpy or a close friend snaps at you for no reason? Those are more difficult to brush off, of course. However, just because they are directed at us, doesn't mean they are *about* us. The other person could have had a rough day, a bad dream, a nagging pain, or be feeling worried or anxious about something unrelated to you. Chances are that if it seems like they are acting this way "for no reason," it is a reason that has nothing to do with you.

Here's the thing. You can choose to take these things personally if you want, but you are setting yourself up for potentially unnecessary anxiety, hurt, or anger—all of which take a lot of energy. You'll be much better off if you can slow down, take a deep breath, and make a fair evaluation of the situation. After that, if you're still not sure whether or not it is personal, why not err on the side of least anxiety? Just assume it is not about you and save that energy for more enjoyable things!

Habit #7
Practice Optimism

Expect good things. Believe that success is possible. Hope for the best.

Some people think this approach to life is foolish. They claim you are only setting yourself up for disappointment. Yet, while it is true that pessimists are less surprised by their disappointments, they don't suffer any fewer of them. They just miss out on the pleasure of looking forward to the good things that can and do happen all the time.

More importantly, studies have shown that optimists generally live longer and happier lives than pessimists. What's not to like about that?

Of course, very few people actually admit to being pessimists. Instead, they claim to be "realists." I suppose that argument applies if you are looking at statistical probabilities, but just because something is improbable doesn't mean it is *impossible*. Back in the 1940s, everyone assumed it was impossible to run a mile in less than four minutes. Roger Bannister didn't assume that. In fact, he believed it was not only possible but that he was the guy to do it. Sure enough, in May of 1954, he broke the four-minute mile.

We hear all the time about people who overcome incredible odds to achieve their dreams. Do you think they wake up in the morning convinced they are going to fail? No!

Most of us don't have goals as lofty or seemingly impossible as Roger Bannister's. In my opinion, that is all the more reason for us to practice optimism!

Yes, it is statistically unlikely that you will be promoted. There are fewer supervisors at each level than there are supervisees. Still, people get promoted. Why not you? People get raises, too. Why not you? People get good deals, occasionally. Why not you? Why not now? It is also possible that you'll make the green light, find a parking space, get a compliment from a customer or co-worker, finish that project on time, get a good night's sleep, etc. If it is possible, then it *can* happen. Next time you are thinking about the future, imagine the best outcome and ask yourself "Why not?" At the very least, it will make you feel better about life and about the future.

Here is another reason why optimists have a happier life. They tend to be more successful. You see, if you believe that a goal is attainable, you are more likely to help make it happen. Using the promotion example above, which person is more likely to exert extra effort to get a promotion: someone who believes it is possible or someone who has given up hope? In a more common scenario, if you believe you are going to have a good day, you are more likely to smile at strangers, have more patience with the barista, etc. The result? People smile back. The barista is nice. Before you know it, you *are* having a good day! You have just created your own success simply by believing it to be possible. Pretty amazing, eh?

If you ask me, a little disappointment now and then is a small price to pay for a longer, happier, and more successful life. Give it a try!

Habit #8

Just Do It

This isn't about what you *should* do. This is about those tasks that you've already decided to do but keep putting off—either because you don't really want to do them or because they will take more than an hour or so of concentrated effort. You know how it is. You decide before you go to bed that you are definitely going to do this tomorrow. Then, tomorrow comes and you just never get around to it. Maybe you're:

- Too tired—In fact, just the thought of doing this makes you tired!
- Too busy—It is amazing how many things keep coming up that are more important than this.
- Not ready—You need to get all of the little stuff out of the way so you can concentrate on this better.

Whatever the reason, putting off the task is a bad idea for the simple reason that it gives you more time to agonize over it. You are probably going to blame this agony on the task itself, which is not entirely inappropriate. However, your delay makes it much worse. For one thing, you end up spending way more time thinking about it than you ever would have spent doing it. Plus, you end up feeling guilty or berating yourself for putting it off, which adds to your misery.

Here's an example of how this can happen:

I needed to re-caulk my bathtub. Caulking a bathtub isn't the easiest task for most of us, anyway, and the main reason I needed to do it was that I'd made such a mess of it the last time I did it. In my own defense, there were some unusual challenges involved in this project (e.g. big gaps and drifting sand from behind the walls), and I wasn't looking forward to confronting them again. Still, this was something I really needed to do. I thought about it every time I looked at the tub. I actually put it on my to-do list several times prior to visits from out-of-towners, but I never managed to get to it. Instead, I suffered the embarrassment of having them see messy caulk when they used the shower or bath. *This went on for at least three years!* I finally tackled the job earlier this year. It wasn't easy. The challenges were every bit as challenging as I expected. It took me about twelve hours, over two days. Happily, it was well worth the effort. My bathtub looks great!

Even though this turned out to be a big job, the twelve hours I spent on it paled in comparison to all of the hours I spent wondering how to do it, feeling guilty about not doing it, agonizing over how to fit it into my schedule, worrying about what people were thinking when they saw it, etc. What a waste!

Being a born procrastinator, I have to remind myself to "Just Do It" fairly often, even for small jobs. Usually, it is a difficult or unpleasant work task. Sometimes, though, it can be something as simple as forcing myself to deal with a household chore today instead of waiting until tomorrow.

If you've got one or more tasks or projects that you are putting off, ask yourself if the delay is really worth the anxiety and/or guilt you are experiencing. If not, then just do it—and make more room in your mind for pleasant thoughts and more room in your life for joy.

Habit #9

Choose Your Attitude

You can't change your past. You've got only so much control over your future. And, if you are like most of us, you have to do things every week that you'd rather not do. All of that could lead to a decidedly unhappy life.

However, there is one area over which you have total control. You can choose how you respond to activities, events, and other people. The choice you make can often influence the outcome. More importantly, it can determine the level of enjoyment you experience in the process.

Here are a couple of examples of how the right attitude can make a difference:

My job requires me to be on-call for computer system emergencies. For some reason, these calls frequently happen at the most inconvenient times (while out to dinner with a friend, when I'm pressed for time to be somewhere or get something done, on my first day to relax after three busy weeks, etc.). Before returning these calls, I have learned the importance of reminding myself that this customer is depending on me to get him or her out of a jam that isn't his or her fault any more than it is mine. I also tell myself not to worry because it might just turn out to be an easy fix that won't take very long. This attitude "adjustment" makes for a much more pleasant experience for both of us. It also helps me to focus more on the problem at hand instead of how soon I can get off the phone. This often, ironically, leads to a faster solution and thus, less time on the phone!

I had dinner recently with someone who went through some pretty rough times in her late teens and early twenties. As we talked about this, it was clear that she would have preferred to have avoided this adversity. However, she opted for an attitude of determination to overcome it, instead of feeling victimized by it. Her attitude (plus a lot of hard work, of course) helped her to succeed. She hasn't stopped there, though. When looking back on that adversity, she chooses to focus on what she learned instead of what she suffered. That attitude frees her to enjoy the life she lives now and provides a foundation for much more success in the future.

Choosing the right attitude can make a real difference in many aspects of your life. Next time you are feeling resentful or irritable about something or someone, try an attitude adjustment. It will help you to have a better (and happier) experience, and just might result in a better outcome, too!

Habit #10

Experience the Moments

Days, weeks, and years go by. Each of those days, weeks, and years—and ultimately, your entire life—is made up of individual moments. This advice is about experiencing each of those moments instead of cruising through them on auto-pilot, as we often do.

There are several components to this:

First, you have to appreciate the value of living in the present. As John Lennon sang, "Life is what happens to you while you're busy making other plans." Recognize that your life is what is happening *right now*, whether you like it or not. Pay attention or you might miss it! This doesn't mean that you can't plan for a different or better future, but not at the expense of dismissing what *is*, as though it doesn't count. Every minute counts! Living in the present helps to reduce stress, too. The more time you spend focusing on the here and now, the less time you have to be stressed or anxious about the future (or the past).

Second, you have to avoid multi-tasking—at least if more than one of the tasks requires that your brain be engaged. Although you can physically text one person while talking to another, there is some part of that "simultaneous" action that is not getting all of your attention. The same goes for finishing a proposal while talking to your significant other on the phone, listening to anything but background music while doing office work, and watching TV while talking to your kids. What? You don't have time to single-task? If you want quality results, you don't really have any other option.

Going even deeper, make sure you experience the moments in your one-on-one conversations. Focus on what the other person is saying and how they are saying it—instead of assuming it is the same old thing, or thinking about something else entirely, or missing part of what is being said because you are too busy focusing on what you are going to say in response. Many of the best parts of your life are going to be about relationships—family, friends, co-workers, and others. Paying attention to what these people say to you goes a long way towards deepening and nurturing those relationships.

Finally, pay attention to the little things in life—the interesting flavors in your evening meal, the flowers blooming by the side of road, how fresh the air smells after it rains, how good it feels to hug a loved one.

Experiencing the moments of your life helps you to enjoy a deeper, richer, and more rewarding life. Give it a try!

One More Thing

Please remember that just knowing about these ten habits isn't going to make you any happier. You have to *practice the habits* in order to have a happier life.

I promise you that if you do that, you will find yourself...

    smiling more often,

        enjoying life more,

            feeling better about yourself,

                and happily living a happier life!

About the Author

Lynda K. Giddens is a part-time blogger and full-time small business owner. She lives in Seattle, Washington.

This is the first in a series of books on happiness. For more information about Lynda, more insights into happiness, and news of upcoming books, please visit her website, www.BrighterLifeIdeas.com.

www.ingramcontent.com/pod-product-compliance
Lightning Source LLC
Chambersburg PA
CBHW061348040426
42444CB00011B/3145